Why do dolphins squeak?

First published as hardback in 2006 by Miles Kelly Publishing Ltd, Bardfield Centre, Great Bardfield, Essex, CM7 4SLCopyright © Miles Kelly Publishing Ltd 2006

This 2009 edition published and distributed by:

Mason Crest Publishers Inc.
370 Reed Road, Broomall, Pennsylvania 19008
(866) MCP-BOOK (toll free)
www.masoncrest.com

Why Why Why—
Do Dolphins Squeak?
ISBN 978-1-4222-1581-4
Library of Congress Cataloging-in-Publication data is available

Why Why Why—?
Complete 23 Title Series
ISBN 978-1-4222-1568-5

Printed in the United States of America

Contents

What is the biggest whale?

The blue whale is the biggest whale. In fact it is the biggest animal ever to have lived. Some grow up to 100 feet long – the same as 18 people swimming end-to-end. Like all whales, the blue whale spends its entire life in water.

Remember

How long can a bottlenose whale hold its breath? Read these pages again if you can't remember.

4

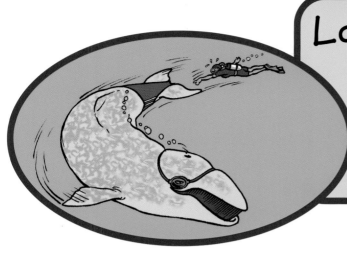

How heavy is a whale?

Very heavy! Some whales, such as killer whales and minke whales, reach up to 10 tons in weight. This isn't as heavy as the blue whale, which weighs a massive 150 tons — that's the weight of 35 elephants!

Blue whale

Can whales breathe under water?

No, they can't. Whales breathe air through a blowhole on the top of their head. They have to hold their breath when they dive underwater to feed, then come back to the surface for air. The bottlenose whale can hold its breath for more than one hour!

What is a dolphin?

A dolphin is a mammal that lives in the sea and some rivers. They come to the surface to breathe air. Dolphins are excellent swimmers and can often be seen leaping above the waves. There are about 35 types of dolphin and most grow to 10 feet in length.

Bottlenose dolphins

Faster, faster!

The fin whale can swim at 12 miles per hour, making it one of the fastest whales. It is also the second largest whale, reaching 85 feet in length!

Can dolphins smell?

Dolphins have little or no sense of smell. They use taste to tell them about the foods they eat. They can taste the water too, to see if there might be any other bits of food drifting nearby!

Draw

On a piece of paper, draw a dolphin outline and color it in any pattern you wish. Give your dolphin a name.

What is a porpoise?

Porpoises are mammals that look similar to dolphins. However, porpoises are smaller and grow to around 6 feet or less. There are six types of porpoise, which all live in the sea. Porpoises have spade-shaped teeth, unlike dolphins, which have cone-shaped teeth.

Spectacled porpoise

Why do whales splash backwards?

Whales jump out of the sea and crash down backwards as a way of sending messages to other whales. This is called breaching. They may also splash backwards to get rid of barnacles that stick to their skin. Even humpback whales can breach — and they weigh 30 tons!

Breaching humpback whale

Think

Barnacles are a type of shellfish. Can you think of any other creatures that live in shells?

Which dolphin is almost blind?

The Indus River dolphin lives in rivers in India. It has tiny eyes and is almost blind because the water is so muddy. To find its way in the water, it drags its flipper along the riverbed.

Indus River dolphin

Why do barnacles stick to whales?

Barnacles are a type of shellfish that stick to moving whales. They can catch more of their favorite food — tiny shrimps and plants called plankton — when they are on the move.

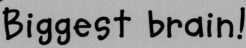

Biggest brain!

The sperm whale has the biggest brain in the world! It weighs 18 pounds and is five times bigger than a human brain. However, the sperm whale is not the cleverest animal.

Do dolphins live in schools?

Many kinds of dolphin live in groups called schools. Bottlenose dolphins live in small groups of two to four animals, but common dolphins live in bigger groups, sometimes of over 2,000. Occasionally, many kinds of dolphin join together to form even bigger groups of many thousands.

Swim

When you go swimming see if you can move like a dolphin. Keep your legs together and wave them up and down.

Why are dolphins so clever?

Dolphins have large brains, which means they are clever, intelligent animals. They can learn tricks such as leaping through hoops and knocking balls with their noses. They can even solve simple puzzles and count!

ABCDEFGHI
JKLMNOPQR
STUVWXYZ

Why do dolphins squeak?

Dolphins use squeaking sounds to talk to each other and to surprise their prey. The sounds bounce off nearby objects and by listening to the echoes that bounce back, the dolphins can work out where things are.

Common dolphins

Rescue me!

There are stories of dolphins saving people in danger in the sea. The dolphins might nudge them to shore, and some stories even tell of dolphins protecting people from sharks!

Why do whales puff and blow?

Whales puff and blow when they breathe. Whales, dolphins and porpoises breathe through a blowhole on top of their head, instead of through a nose. When a whale surfaces, it pushes old air, and a slimy liquid called mucus, out through its blowhole. This is called a "blow."

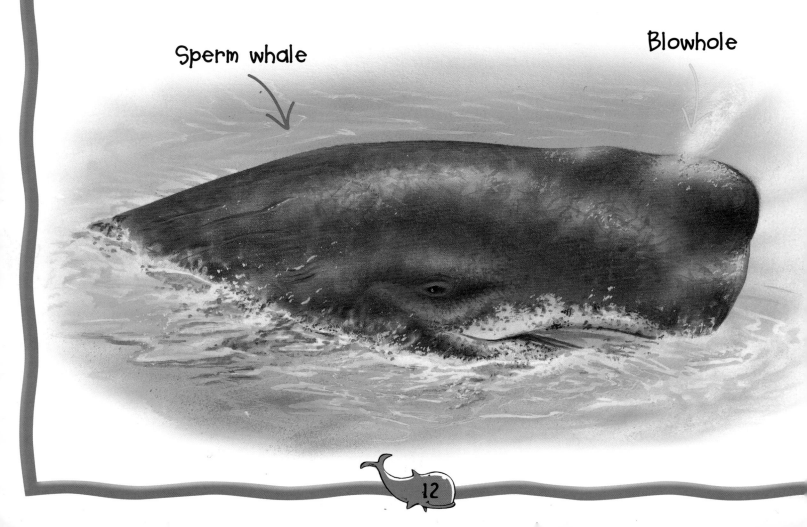

Sperm whale

Blowhole

Sperm whale diving

Which whale dives the deepest?

The sperm whale does. Before diving, the sperm whale comes to the surface to take some deep breaths. Then it arches its back so that its body points straight down. This helps it to plunge quickly into the depths – down to 10,000 feet!

It's a bit blowy!

All whales have 'blows' of different shapes and sizes. The sperm whale's blow is unusual – it is less than 6 feet in height, quite bushy, and angled forwards to the left.

Blow

With a straw, suck up some water but don't swallow it! Aim the straw up and blow the water out like a whale.

What do whales like to eat?

All whales are carnivores, which means that they eat other animals. There are two types of whale – baleen and toothed. Baleen whales eat tiny shrimps called krill. Toothed whales eat mainly fish, and some even crunch up crabs and shellfish!

Are whales and dolphins like people?

Whales, dolphins and porpoises are mammals, just like people. They are warm-blooded like us and have the same parts inside their bodies, too. They have a skeleton of bones, a stomach, a heart to pump blood and lungs to breathe air.

Inside a dolphin

Whale-size feast!

In summer, blue whales can eat 4 tons of food a day. That's 1.5 million calories – the same as eating 7,350 hamburgers. That's why blue whales are so heavy.

How do whales and dolphins keep warm?

Unlike many mammals, whales and dolphins don't have a thick coat of fur to keep them warm. Instead, they have a thick layer of fat called blubber just under the skin. In large whales the blubber can be more than 20 inches thick!

When did whales walk on land?

About 50 million years ago, whales lived on land. They used their flippers as legs, but slowly over time they lived more in water. The earliest whale was *Pakicetus*, which grew to about 6 feet long. *Pakicetus* could run on land and swim.

Name

Have a look at the big picture. Can you name any of the body parts inside the dolphin?

Pakicetus

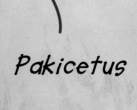

How do dolphins catch fish?

Dolphins use their speedy swimming to catch fish. They twist and turn through the water and snap at their prey. Bottlenose dolphins work together to gather a shoal of fish into a tight group called a "bait-ball." The dolphins dash into the bait-ball and try to grab the fish.

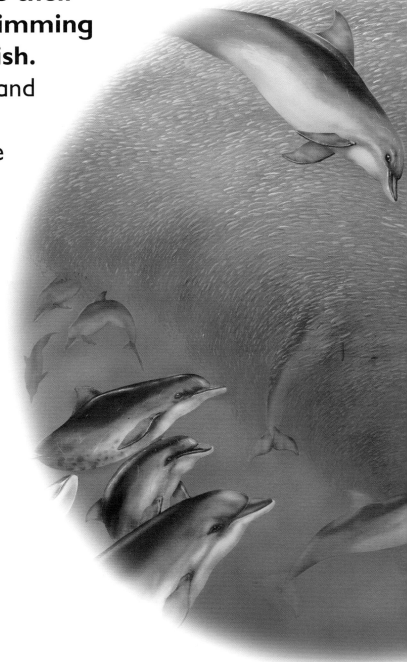

Paint

The sperm whale's favorite food is giant squid. Think about your favorite foods and paint a delicious picture of them.

Which whale eats giant squid?

The sperm whale only eats giant squid, which live in very deep water. To hunt for its favorite food, the sperm whale can hold its breath for more than two hours. The largest giant squid ever caught by a sperm whale was 40 feet long!

Sperm whale

Bait-ball

Melon head!

Dolphins and toothed whales have a "melon" – a large, fluid-filled lump at the front of their head. It helps the animals' squeaks go in the right direction when they are hunting.

What is a group of whales called?

A group of whales is called a pod. Normally there are 20 to 30 whales in a pod. The older females are usually in charge. They decide when to rest, when to hunt and where to travel during the year.

Do all whales have teeth?

Pilot whale

Only "toothed whales," such as sperm whales and pilot whales, have teeth. They are active hunters and feed on squid, fish and other mammals that live in the sea. Some toothed whales only have two teeth. These whales have to suck in their prey and swallow it whole.

Play

Mix some sand with a few marbles. With a friend, see who can sieve the most sand and find the marbles!

Why do whales sieve the sea?

Some whales, such as the humpback whale, sieve the sea for their food of tiny sea creatures called krill. These whales have lots of long, bendy strips called baleen that hang in their mouth. The whale pushes water out through its baleen, which catches food like a giant filter.

Humpback whale →

Big ears!

Hector's dolphin is sometimes called the Mickey Mouse dolphin, because its back fin is shaped like the cartoon character's ears!

Do whales make curtains?

The humpback whale makes "bubble-curtains." It dives down, then swims up slowly in small circles, breathing out as it moves. This creates a curtain of rising bubbles, which keeps krill and other food close together – ready for a big mouthful!

19

Which whale can surf?

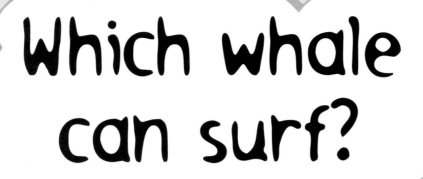

The killer whale can. Killer whales, or orcas, will surf onto a beach by swimming quickly towards the shore, to grab a young seal or sea lion. Then the whale wriggles back into the sea, holding its victim in its sharp, back-curved teeth.

Killer whale

Why do dolphins swim near boats?

Lots of dolphins like to swim in the big waves created by moving boats. This is called bow-riding. People aren't sure why dolphins do this. They may be waiting for leftover food to be thrown overboard, or saving energy by surfing on the ship's wave.

↑ Pacific white-sided dolphin

It's my name!

Humpback whales get their name because of the way they hump their back up out of the water before they dive down into the ocean to feed.

Have a go

What trick can you do? Try patting your head and rubbing your tummy at the same time.

Can dolphins perform tricks?

Yes they can. Many people visit sea-life centers and aquariums to see dolphins performing in shows. When the dolphins are being trained they have been known to change the tricks and invent new puzzles to make them more fun.

Which whales swordfight?

Narwhals do. Only male narwhals have a tusk. They use it to show off and fight with other males during the breeding season, to win over a female. The tusk is actually a very long, sharp tooth that grows in a corkscrew pattern. It can grow up to 10 feet long.

Narwhals fighting

Long in the tusk!

In the 16th century, Queen Elizabeth I received a carved tusk worth £10,000 — the cost of a castle. It was believed to be a unicorn horn, but was actually a narwhal tusk!

Singing humpback whale

Why do whales sing?

Whales 'sing' when they want to find a partner. The male humpback whale sings while hanging in the water with its flippers and tail dangling down. It makes wails, squeaks and shrieks in a pattern that it repeats. This sometimes lasts for up to 22 hours!

Play

Pretend to be a narwhal! Attach a straw to your nose with a piece of blu-tac, as your tusk!

Do whales go on holiday?

Yes, they do, in a way! Whales, dolphins and porpoises go on long journeys at the same time each year — this is called migration. They travel to find the best food. Some whales travel to warmer, calmer waters to give birth.

How big is a baby whale?

Very big! A newborn grey whale, called a calf, is about 16 feet long and weighs half a ton. It grows inside its mother for 13 months before it is born. The blue whale calf is the biggest animal baby – it is 23 feet long and weighs 3 tons at birth!

Do whales and dolphins drink milk?

Yes they do, just like all other mammals. Most feed on their mother's milk for about a year. The milk is rich and full of goodness. The blue whale calf drinks 80 gallons of milk a day – enough to fill four bathtubs!

Dolphin-zilla!

Killer whales are not actually whales, but the biggest members of the dolphin family. Males grow up to 30 feet and weigh 10 tons.

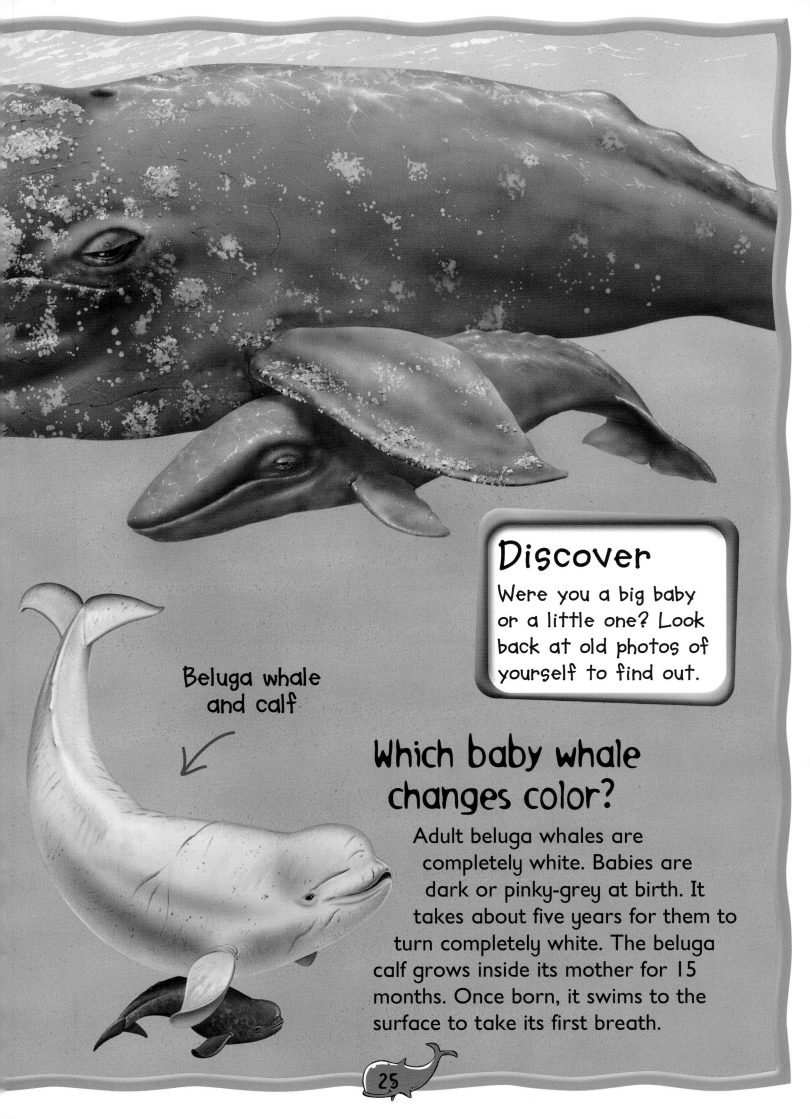

Beluga whale
and calf

Discover

Were you a big baby or a little one? Look back at old photos of yourself to find out.

Which baby whale changes color?

Adult beluga whales are completely white. Babies are dark or pinky-grey at birth. It takes about five years for them to turn completely white. The beluga calf grows inside its mother for 15 months. Once born, it swims to the surface to take its first breath.

Why do dolphins leap?

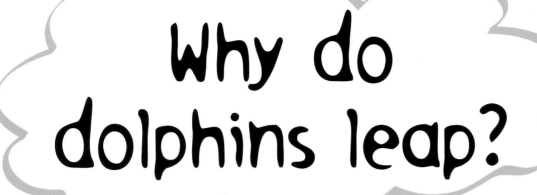

Dolphins leap for several reasons. On long journeys, leaping can save energy — it is much easier to move through air than through water. They might also leap to see fish from above the water, or simply for fun. The dusky dolphin is one of the most impressive leapers!

Dusky dolphin

How do dolphins say hello?

Dolphins rub, stroke and roll over each other to say "hello." Whales, dolphins and porpoises have very sensitive skin. Touching and stroking happens more during breeding time. A mother whale often strokes her baby to give it comfort and warmth.

Atlantic spotted dolphins

Do people go whale watching?

When people are on vacation they may go on boat trips to see whales in their natural surroundings, and scientists watch whales to learn about how they live. Sometimes, whales are frightened or disturbed by this, so it's important to explore their behavior with care.

Do people still hunt whales?

People have hunted whales for thousands of years. Today, some hunting continues, but many whales are now protected. These animals were valuable because their blubber could be burned in lamps, their meat could be eaten and their baleen strips were used for clothing and tools.

Smile!

The bowhead whale has a big mouth. In fact, it has the biggest mouth of any animal. It measures 33 feet around the lips and 20 people could fit inside it!

Whale hunting in the 19th century

Why do whales and dolphins get stranded?

No one knows why whales and dolphins get stranded, or washed up and stuck on the shore. The animals may have been disturbed by storms, become ill or simply got lost.

Who was swallowed by a whale?

In the Bible, a man called Jonah was swallowed by a whale and he lived inside it for three days and three nights. Jonah prayed to God that he would get out of the whale. Eventually, the whale spat Jonah out onto dry land.

Jonah and the whale

Think

There are many different types of whale. Can you name three different whales in this book?

29

Quiz time

page 9

Do you remember what you have read about whales and dolphins? These questions will test your memory. The pictures will help you. If you get stuck, read the pages again.

3. Which dolphin is almost blind?

page 10

page 4

4. Do dophins live in schools?

1. What is the biggest whale?

page 13

5. What do whales like to eat?

page 7

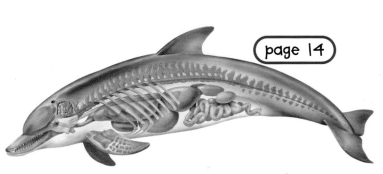

page 14

2. Can dolphins smell?

6. Are whales and dolphins like people?

7. What is a group of whales called?

page 17

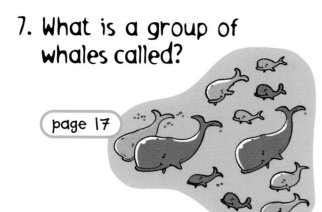

8. Do all whales have teeth?

page 18

9. Which whale can surf?

page 20

10. Do whales and dolphins drink milk?

page 24

11. Which baby whale changes color?

page 25

12. How do dolphins say hello?

page 27

13. Why do whales and dolphins get stranded?

page 29

Answers

1. The blue whale
2. No, not very well
3. The Indus River dolphin
4. Yes, they do
5. Fish, crabs and krill
6. Yes, they are mammals like people
7. A pod
8. Only toothed whales have teeth
9. The killer whale
10. Yes, they do
11. A baby beluga whale
12. They rub, stroke and roll over each other
13. Because they get lost or ill

31

Index